RAILS ACROSS CANADA

A PICTORIAL JOURNEY FROM COAST TO COAST

RAILS ACROSS CANADA

A PICTORIAL JOURNEY FROM COAST TO COAST

DAVID CABLE

PEN & SWORD
TRANSPORT

First published in Great Britain in 2015 by
Pen & Sword Transport
An imprint of Pen & Sword Books Ltd
47 Church Street
Barnsley
South Yorkshire
S70 2AS

ISBN 9781473838062

Printed and bound by Imago Publising Limited.

Pen & Sword Books Ltd incorporates the imprints of Pen & Sword Archaeology,
Atlas, Aviation, Battleground, Discovery, Family History, History, Maritime, Military,
Naval, Politics, Railways, Select, Social History, Transport, True Crime, and Claymore
Press, Frontline Books, Leo Cooper, Praetorian Press, Remember When, Seaforth
Publishing and Wharncliffe.

For a complete list of Pen and Sword titles please contact
Pen and Sword Books Limited
47 Church Street, Barnsley, South Yorkshire, S70 2AS, England
E-mail: enquiries@pen-and-sword.co.uk
Website: www.pen-and-sword.co.uk

DAVID CABLE – OTHER PUBLICATIONS

Railfreight in Colour (for the modeller and historian)

BR Passenger Sectors in Colour (for the modeller and historian)

Lost Liveries of Privatisation in Colour (for the modeller and historian)

Hydraulics in the West

The Blue Diesel Era

Rails across America – A Pictorial Journey across the USA

Introduction

The Canadian railway system is dominated by two privately owned companies, Canadian National (CN) and Canadian Pacific (CP), although CN was publicly owned until 1995. These companies form two of the big six North American class 1 railroad operators. Both railways span most of the country, CP operating from Montreal to Vancouver via Toronto, Winnipeg and Calgary, whilst CN stretches from Halifax in Nova Scotia to Vancouver, taking the more northerly route via Edmonton in Alberta. CP has a further line to the south across the prairie states from Winnipeg through Lethbridge.

All these lines have to negotiate the various mountain ranges in the west, CP being famous for the Kicking Horse Pass over the Rocky Mountains, with the Crow's Nest Pass to the south. CN surmounted the range using the Yellowhead Pass, which was originally recommended when the CP was built, being an easier route than that selected, but had the disadvantage of being less direct.

Both CN and CP have been involved with several mergers and acquisitions over the years, in order to consolidate their operations, and in particular to gain the companies own access to warm water ports on the Atlantic coast side of North America, since shipping is curtailed in winter by the freezing up of the St Lawrence River.

CP purchased the Delaware & Hudson RR in north eastern USA, which in conjunction with trackage rights, provided access to New York and Philadelphia sea ports, and acquired SOO line, which with the subsequent takeover of Dakota, Minnesota and Eastern RR and Iowa, Chicago and Eastern, provided the means to operate on its own tracks to Chicago and Kansas City, and also the potential to gain access to the huge coal reserves in the Powder river area in Wyoming.

CN was even more aggressive. From its subsidiary the Duluth, Winnipeg and Pacific, it developed via the Wisconsin Central (which had taken over Algoma Central, which operated north from Sault Ste. Marie into Ontario) giving access to Chicago, and then the major purchase of the Illinois Central, which resulted in a system covering from across Canada down to the Gulf of Mexico. Interestingly, as a result of its takeover of Wisconsin Central, it also found itself owning English, Welsh and Scottish Railways in the UK, which Wisconsin Central had established in 1997 to operate most of the British freight traffic. This was sold off to the German railway operator DB Schenker in 2007.

Within Canada other mergers by CN included taking over BC Rail, a substantial company covering British Columbia, and the Northern Alberta lines. A number of smaller companies are active in addition to the big two. The Goderich and Exeter is a short line owned by the Rail America group; Ontario Northern and Ontario Southern work within that province, but the railways on Prince Edward Island and Newfoundland closed being unremunerative. There are four privately owned major ore carrying lines in eastern Quebec and Labrador, all working north from Sept Iles in Quebec province, at the mouth of the St Lawrence, but quite divorced from the rest of Canada's railways. These are the Arnaud, Quebec Cartier, Quebec, North Shore & Labrador, and the Wabush Lake, of which the QNSL also operates a passenger train service.

Passenger train operations in Canada are, like the USA, relatively sparse. VIA is the principal operator, using the tracks of CN and CP. The major cities in the east – Toronto, Montreal, Quebec, Windsor and Ottawa, etc. are inter-connected, and services run through to Halifax and Gaspe in the north eastern maritime areas. But, recognising the distances involved, the only cross-Canada service, the 'Canadian' takes 3 days to complete its journey, and only travels twice each week each way (three times in summer). It is still a classic North American train with dome cars and an observation car at the rear. Another interesting VIA route is that from Winnipeg to Churchill on Hudson Bay, operating twice a week each way and taking about 36 hours for the trip.

A further VIA service is from Jasper to Prince Rupert on the Pacific coast.

There are regular commuter style services in the Toronto area (GO Transit), Montreal (AMT) and Vancouver (West Coast Express). A few other services include a BC Rail (now CN) railcar service between Vancouver and Lillooet, a currently suspended VIA service from Victoria to Courtenay on Vancouver Island, the former Northlander of Ontario Northern RR from Toronto to Cochrane, and the current Polar Bear Express from Cochrane to Moosonee.

Special Tourist trains include the Agawa Canyon train of the Algoma Central, and in particular, The Rocky Mountaineer which runs in two parts from Calgary and Jasper in Alberta, to Vancouver BC, having joined at Kamloops BC, where an overnight stop is made.

American incursions are made into Canada. Burlington Northern Santa Fe have a line into Vancouver from Washington State, and there is a short Union Pacific branch into southern British Columbia. On the northern side of Lake Erie, a CSX line (formerly NYC) runs in principle between Buffalo and Detroit providing a secondary route between these two cities. Three US Amtrak passenger services also work between Canadian and American cities. The Cascades is a service on the west coast between Vancouver and Eugene OR, serving Seattle and Portland. The Maple Leaf operates between Toronto and New York City via Niagara Falls and Buffalo, and the Adirondack between Montreal and New York City via the D&H line through Albany NY.

However, the principal traffic in Canada is freight, and in particular coal, grain, and intermodal traffic in containers, whilst there is also some mixed freight (manifest trains). Although, in the eastern part of the country, freight trains that do not travel west are often relatively small, especially on the shorter lines, those travelling trans-continental, and particularly the coal trains from the mines in Alberta and British Columbia are very substantial, requiring multi-locomotive haulage.

Locomotives are all of US manufacture by both Electro Motive Division (formerly General Motors) and especially now General Electric. Few first generation diesel locomotives are now in use, but second generation engines from the 1970/1980 era with horsepower in the 3000–3600 range are still widespread in use on freight trains in the flatter parts of the country, although CN still makes use of them assisting higher powered locos in the mountain areas.

Third generation engines of up to 4400 HP now predominate in the mountain areas, as well as on trans-continental traffic, but interestingly CP uses AC traction almost exclusively whereas CN is primarily a DC railroad.

Passenger locomotives operated by VIA are mainly the EMD F40PH-2 type, working in multiple on trains such as the Canadian, but the newer GE P32B-9 is seen in increasing numbers in the Quebec to Windsor corridor. Commuter services employ a variety of second and third generation passenger classes.

Train operations follow similar practices adopted in other large countries, such as the USA and Australia, where pioneers developed the land and the railways followed, and centres of population were often widespread. Thus tracks tended to be single with passing loops at regular intervals, but whilst this was generally satisfactory in the early days, with the growth of traffic to the present day, double tracking has become necessary in many cases given the restrictions that terrain may impose.

Historically, the Canadian Pacific line was constructed through to the west as a concession to encourage British Columbia to join the other provinces to form what is now the Dominion of Canada. The engineering of the line was a highly complex and dangerous undertaking through the mountains. The line generally tried to follow river valleys where possible, but the canyons of the Thompson and Fraser rivers necessitated cutting into the sides, which restricted the means of providing sufficient passing loops, and in turn restricted line capacity.

The Canadian National, which was formed from a number of government controlled bankrupt lines including the Grand Trunk, also included lines to the west coast. These had taken a more northerly route across the prairie states and into the Rocky Mountains, but then swung south to Kamloops BC where the CP was already established. Because the CP had been the first line to meet the challenges of the canyons, and its surveyors had chosen the better sides of the river to construct the line, the CN was forced to use the opposite banks in most cases from Kamloops west, also having the same restrictions on traffic capacity.

In the 21st century, the two lines agreed to adopt uni-directional operations through the major restricted areas, whereby trains heading south and west used one track, and those working north and east used the other, providing a massive increase in capacity. This arrangement applies from just south of Ashcroft BC down to near Mission. A similar arrangement was also adopted in Ontario between Reynolds, just south of Parry Sound, and Wanup, just south of Sudbury.

This book of photographs endeavours to show the railroads of Canada from east to west and in all the seasons. I make no excuse for the fact that the great bulk of photos show trains in the mountains – the scenery is just too good. Also included is a selection of photos showing Canadian locos working in the USA and shots of some of the trains acquired by the two class 1 companies in the US.

Shots are also included of acquired US locos working through in Canada.

The majority of the photos are of my own taking, during trips I made to the Vancouver area in 1991, 1999 and 2001, an extended trip with Ian Francis (see below) when we followed the lines from Banff to Vancouver in 2006, and trips in the Toronto area in 1994 and 2005. But great help and pictures have been provided by good friends, namely Ian Francis, a tour manager with Great Rail Journeys, John Chalcraft who runs Rail Photoprints (www.railphotoprints.zenfolio.com), Colin Marsden, who likes the snow and runs The Railway Centre, (www.railway-centre.com) and David Brace, who on a business trip was taken into the Victoria bridge at Montreal as a favour for having endured three solid days of meetings! My thanks to all four of you.

This book has brought back happy memories of spectacular trips, and of some most helpful railway staff and other members of the public.

David Cable
Hartley Wintney
Hants
October 2014

Four Alco RS18s, headed by 905, haul an Arnaud Railroad ore train towards the coast across the Canadian Shield at Point Noire, PQ in July 1994. (DC Collection)

The Quebec Cartier Railroad is another ore handling system in Quebec province. Approaching Charles passing siding, M636 86 leads two others through the wilderness with a train of empties returning to the mines in October 1994. (DC Collection)

A pair of CN GP39-2s shunt the dock area at Halifax NS in May 2007. The passenger station is out of sight to the left of the picture. (Ian Francis)

A sight typical of North American trains; a rear end observation car tails the rear of the VIA 1215 train to Montreal seen leaving Halifax NS in June 2009. (Ian Francis)

A pair of New Brunswick Southern GP9s, 3735 and 3757, are not overtaxed hauling a single box car at McAdam NB, August 1998. (DC Collection)

VIA train No 17 from Montreal arrives at its destination Gaspe PQ behind F40PH-2 6404 in August 2003. (DC Collection)

Watched by passers-by as it crosses the bridge, VIA P42-9 907 is seen arriving at Quebec with the 0825 service from Montreal, May 2007. (Ian Francis)

With the Chateau overlooking the scene, the same loco, 907, leaves Quebec with the 1235 train to Montreal that same day after a quick turn round. (Ian Francis)

CN C44-9W 2600 heads a manifest freight train heading north across the Victoria bridge which crosses the St Lawrence River at Montreal in October 2007. (David Brace)

Track workers keep clear as the 'Adirondack' operated by Amtrak from Montreal to New York City heads south across the Victoria bridge at Montreal in October 2007. The train is powered by class P42B-9 number 43. (David Brace)

VIA has decorated a number of its class F40PH-2 locomotives in various advertising schemes, ranging from commercial products to films. This striking example for Budweiser and the NFL Super Bowl is seen on 6424 in Ottawa ON in November 1985. (DC Collection)

VIA F40PHM-2 6401 in Spiderman livery passes Pickering, on the outskirts of Toronto with train No 44 from Toronto to Ottawa in February 2009. (Colin Marsden)

One of the latest VIA passenger class locomotives, P42-9 907 has been held outside Toronto Union station by a signal check, and now accelerates to bring its Montreal to Toronto service into its destination, October 2005.

GO F59PH 535 tails the service from Pickering to Oakville seen entering Toronto Union station in June 1994. This train is worked on a push-pull system with a driving coach at the other end.

Difficulty in getting from one platform to another at Toronto restricted my ability to get a closer photo than this, but the train is of sufficient interest to include this photo. The train is an LRC (Light – Rapid – Comfortable) service from Toronto to Montreal headed by engine 6905.

The view from the CN Tower shows the track layout on the west side of Toronto Union station, with six GO trains stabled in the sidings waiting for the evening rush hour services. This view was not taken from the normal viewing platform, which was closed, but from the less used gallery another 300 feet above. Taken on a less than sunny day in June 1994.

Showing the full height of the
CN Tower and other major
structures in downtown Toronto,
CN GP9 4117 runs light engine
in October 2005.

Ontario Northland FP7 1501 stands at the head of the 'Northlander', awaiting departure from Toronto Union station in June 1994.

It is unusual to see a full length freight train passing through the Union station in Toronto, but Ian Francis got this shot in September 2011. Heading a train of auto racks are CN SD75I 5722, C44-9W 2623 and GP38-2W 4784. (Ian Francis)

A GO train from Burlington ON approaches Toronto behind F59PH 545, one coach bearing an advertising livery. The date is October 2005. The view of this junction is taken from the Bathurst Street Bridge.

One of the newest class of GO locos, the MP40PH-3C, No 646 passes Sunnyside with a 10 car set of empty double deck stock from Mimico to Toronto Union, February 2014. (Colin Marsden)

Stabled at Mimico ON in June 1994, and seen from a passing train, are withdrawn GO engines FP7m 901, F7B 800, another F7B and another FP7m.

CN GP40-2W, ex UP SD40-2 6098 and SD40-2 6000 head west at Bayview Junction near Hamilton ON with an intermodal working, June 1994

Taking the left-hand branch, CP C424 4223, Helm ex GTI GP40 509, CP C424 4224 and RS18 1848 pass through Bayview junction and head towards Hamilton with a manifest freight train, June 1994.

With the CN Bayview sign clearly identifying the location, a CN freight train of auto racks heads west towards the London ON area. In charge are SD40-2W 5337, ex UP SD40-2 6102 and GP40-2W 9656, June 1994.

Another view at Bayview Junction shows a westbound manifest freight in June 1994. In the fairly short lived North American map colour scheme, GP 40-2W 9677 and SD40-2 6007 lead a conventional coloured M636 2323.

Framed by the signals, CN M420W 3516 passes Bayview Junction with a Hamilton bound train of box cars, June 1994.

Also framed by the signals and Hamilton area bound in June 1994, a manifest freight is powered by CN GP40-2W 9646, GT GP38AC 6212, GT GP38 6204 and CN GP40-2W 9400.
This photo shows an example of locos of a CN subsidiary line working outside its own system, which has become more and more common over the years.

CN GP9RM 4130 and GP38-2W 4761 are seen near Komoka ON with the daily London to Windsor local freight, February 2014. (Colin Marsden)

CP 6223, ICE 6415 and CP 6240 pass Amiens Road, west of London ON with a westbound twin stack/auto rack train. (Colin Marsden)

VIA F40PH-2 6411 passes Pulham Road, south of London with train 71 from Toronto to Windsor in less than warm conditions in February 2014. (Colin Marsden)

In an earlier colour scheme, the same engine VIA F40PH-2 6411 carries Operation Lifesaver colours and is seen passing Komoka Junction, west of London ON with train 73 from Toronto to Windsor in February 2009. (Colin Marsden)

A pair of Ontario Southern SW1200s, 1244 and 1245 pass Coakley Bridge, Woodstock ON with empty auto racks from Carney Plant to the OSR sidings at Woodstock, January 2014. (Colin Marsden)

An Ontario Northland manifest freight is seen at Earlton ON in August 1999, behind two SD75ls, 2100 and 2103, SD40-2 1731 and GP38-2 1808. (DC collection)

The Goderich and Exeter line, now owned by the Genesse & Wyoming group, has its terminal on Lake Huron, where three of its GP9s, with 179 leading, stand in the pouring rain at the dockside. The Laker, with its characteristic bridge in the bow, moored alongside waits patiently in September 1993.

One hardly expects to see an engine from Florida in snow! However, Florida East Coast 709 (an ex UP loco) and Helm 6522 climb the bank with grain cars from the harbour at Goderich ON towards the town itself in February 2010. (Colin Marsden)

Goderich & Exeter GP38-2 2303, GP40 4095 and GP38 3821 in various colours pass Mitchell ON with the daily Stratford to Goderich pick up freight, February 2014. (Colin Marsden)

Canada in the winter! The train seen in the previous picture gets to grips with a snow drift at West Park Road near Seaforth ON. (Colin Marsden)

A westbound intermodal service crosses Parry Sound ON behind CP SD40-2F 9012, GP9 1690 and SD40-2Fs 9024 and 9003, November 2009. (John Chalcraft)

VIA F40PH-2s 6407 and 6410 make a scheduled stop at Hornepayne ON in November 2009, as they traverse the country with train no 1, the 'Canadian'. (John Chalcraft)

VIA F40PH-2s 6433, 6434 and 6438 are refuelled at Sioux Lookout in May 2005, whilst in charge of the 'Canadian'. (Ian Francis)

With Winnipeg MB as a backdrop, CN ES44DC 2294 and an SD70M-2 ease out of Transcona yard with an eastbound manifest freight in November 2009. (John Chalcraft)

VIA F40PH-2s 6413 and 6456 rumble across the Assiniboine River Bridge on the approach to Winnipeg station with empty stock for the train to Churchill, October 2009. (John Chalcraft)

VIA F40PH-2s 6413 and 6456 leave Winnipeg Union station with the empty stock from the 'Hudson Bay' ex Churchill, November 2009. (John Chalcraft)

VIA F40PH-2 6445 heads the 'Hudson Bay' from Churchill to Winnipeg at Dauphin MB in November 2009. (John Chalcraft)

Hudson Bay SD50s 5001 and 5004 approach Wabowden MB with the last grain train to Churchill, before the port is closed by ice for the winter, November 2008. (John Chalcraft)

One o'clock in the morning and −16C in November 2008 at Churchill MB where VIA F40PH-2 6445 waits to return to Winnipeg. (John Chalcraft)

CN SD40-2 5370 and SD40-2W 5298 pass through Winnipeg with a local trip freight in November 2008. (John Chalcraft)

A westbound twin stack passes Oakville MB behind CN SD75I 5689 and C44-9W 2636, November 2009. (John Chalcraft)

CP 1128 and 3028 pass Portage La Prairie with a local trip freight from Winnipeg to the Simplot Food processing facility west of Portage, November 2009. (John Chalcraft)

Railink GP9-4 4003, backed by a variety of CP locos, stands in the yard at Ogden shops, Calgary, AB in September 1999.

Freshly painted CP SW900 6711 shows off the new beaver crest being introduced at that time. Seen at Ogden shops, Calgary in September 1999.

CP GP38-2 3130 is fitted out with winterization hatches and poses in the sun at Ogden shops yard in September 1999.

CP SD90MACs 9105 and 9150 plus CW44AC 8522 rush past the station at Banff AB with a mixed TOFC/twin stack intermodal service in September 1999.

Shortly afterwards CP CW44ACs 9596 and 9613 head east with a train of empty grain cars
September 1999.

A pair of CP CW44ACs 9612 and 9360 head west past the station at Banff in June 2014, with a twin stack working. (Ian Francis)

CP CW44ACs 8553 and 9556 snake round the bends of the Bow River at Morant's Curve, near Lake Louise AB, with an eastbound train of empty grain cars in August 2006. This location is named after the official CP photographer, who took many pictures here advertising the scenes viewed from their trains.

A well loaded train of containers climbs towards Morant's Curve on its way to the summit over the Rocky Mountains at Kicking Horse Pass. The train is seen in August 2006, headed by CP SD90MAC 9107 and CW44AC 9585.

The Rocky Mountaineer tourist service from Calgary follows the Bow River at Morant's Curve AB in August 2006, behind GP40-2s 8012 and 8015. At Kamloops BC it will join its sister service which will have started from Jasper AB, and the combined train will terminate in Vancouver.

A westbound grain train is dwarfed by the mountains at Kicking Horse Pass. The train is headed by CP SD40-2 5577 plus two others, and is seen in September 1983. (DC collection)

CEFX CW44AC 1056, CP ES44AC 8716 and CW44AC 9666 do a spot of switching at Field BC in August 2006.

CP CW44AC 9628 and ES44AC 8706 stand in the yard at Field BC with an eastbound train of empty potash cars, August 2006.

The Rocky Mountaineer seen previously at Morant's Curve, is now pictured descending the gorge at Glenogle BC, on the descent between Field and Golden, August 2006.

Golden BC is where the line from Calgary/Banff meets the line, which follows the Columbia River down to Crowsnest Pass, and hosts a locomotive shed. On shed are two CP SD40-2s 6610 and 5757, which display the beaver symbol and a rather tatty version of the twin flag CP Rail System colours, August 2006.

A train of coal empties leaves the yard at Golden and starts its journey south with CP CW44AC 9737 in the lead………..

..........whilst at the rear, banker CP CW44AC 9707 is now able to relax having done its job helping the train over the mountain ranges from Vancouver, August 2006.

CP CW44AC 9596 runs alongside Columbia Lake BC with a train of empty coal hoppers towards Crowsnest in June 2000. (John Chalcraft)

CP SD40-2 5723 leads five other locos including UP CW44AC 6601 with a coal train heading towards Crowsnest Pass and are seen near Lundbreck Falls AB, on their way to Golden, October 1999. (DC Collection)

CEFX CW44AC 1054 and CP CW44AC 9837 enter the yards at Golden BC with a westbound twin stack container service in August 2006. Not much spare capacity on this train.

Running log hood forward, CP SD40-2 5747 ambles past KC Junction at Golden with a short train of potash cars plus caboose, August 2006.

CP CW44AC 9766 heads a train of coal empties, which will take the Crowsnest line at KC Junction, August 2006.

At the rear of this train is banker CW 44AC 9669, showing the huge size of the radiators of these modern GE designed locomotives. The main line to Banff and Calgary carries straight on.

CP CW44ACs 9670 and 9664 pass the signal guarding KC Junction with a westbound coal train almost certainly due for the sea terminal at Roberts Bank, Vancouver, where practically all the coal exports passing through Golden will be sent. Taken at Moberley BC in August 2006.

CP SD90MACs 9107 and 9114 head east at Moberley BC with a fully loaded twin stack container train in August 2006.

A stranger in the CP camp at Forde BC, where CN C44-9W 2541 and CP ES44AC 8712 head east with a train of empty grain cars, August 2006.

A comparison with the picture at KC Junction of engine 9669 shows that the radiator wings of the class ES44AC are even thicker. No 8739 trails a westbound grain train at Forde in August 2006. Note the rear end lamp.

A pair of SD90MACs have another fully loaded twin stack container train in tow, just down the road from Moberley at Forde. In this case Nos 9144 and 9105 are heading west.

The spectacular view at Glacier BC, close to the exit from the Connaught tunnel, where CP CW44AC 8644 heads a westbound potash train past the old station building in August 2006.

The potash train is of such a weight that to surmount the mountains two mid-train helpers are needed, CW44ACs 9567 and 9520.

The westbound Rocky Mountaineer from Calgary passes Glacier in August 2006 on its way to Kamloops and Vancouver behind GP40-2s 8017 and 8016, August 2006.

Climbing up the gradient from Revelstoke, CP CW44ACs 9611 and 9570 labour with their eastbound train of empty potash cars.

CP SD90MACs 9111 and 9110 pass through Revelstoke BC with a westbound train of auto racks and twin stack containers, August 2006.

On the approach to Revelstoke, an eastbound welded rail train crosses the Columbia River, headed by CP CW44AC 9640 in June 2008. (John Chalcraft)

At Watmore BC, a westbound coal train is in charge of CW44ACs 9762 and 9722, with 9707 banking the train at the rear, August 2006.

CEFX 1037 with an eastbound grain train has been parked in the siding at Geddis BC. Have the driver's hours of work reached their limit for the day?

Slightly further along the line at Geddis, three CP CW44ACs, 9708, 9571 and 8521 head east with a manifest freight, a class of train seen infrequently during this visit in August 2006.

CP CW44ACs 9507 and 9578 are held at Tappen BC with their eastbound grain empties, waiting for a westbound manifest freight to clear the single line section, June 2008. (John Chalcraft)

With a real mixture of cars, a westbound manifest freight follows the South Thompson River at Bromley BC in August 2006, behind CP SD90MACs 9127 and 9141. This was a difficult shot to take – the camera kept swinging left to a sandbank in the river where a young lady en deshabille was sunning herself!

Coming the other way from the east at Bromley, a twin stack container train passes with CP CW44ACs 9810 and 9521 doing the honours.

The Canadian Pacific business train passes Bromley with its traditional motive power of heritage units in the old CP livery. The engines are F7A 1400, F7B 1900 and GP38 3084. Taken in June 2000. (John Chalcraft)

CP CW44ACs 9590 and 9507 pass over a crossing at McCracken BC as they head west into Kamloops with a mixed auto rack and twin stack container train in August 2006.

The CP station at Kamloops BC hosts an auto rack/twin stack container train heading west behind three CW44ACs, CEFX 1032, CP 8544 and CEFX 1037. SD90MAC 9127 stands alongside, August 2006.

VIA F40PH-2s 6439 and 6411 make a late evening stop at Saskatoon SK with train no 1, the westbound 'Canadian' in June 2014. (Ian Francis)

In the newest VIA colour scheme F40PH-2 6454 with train no 2, the eastbound 'Canadian', stops at Saskatoon in September 2010. (Ian Francis)

CN C44-9W 2578 plus two others hauling a manifest freight train near Entwhistle AB, west of Edmonton, are seen from the 'Canadian' as it passes by in December 2008. (Ian Francis)

In a spectacular Rocky Mountain vista, CN C44-9Ws 2527, 2506 and SD50F 5413 pass Swan Landing AB with an eastbound manifest freight train in June 2001. (John Chalcraft)

Four Northern Alberta C30-7s 1005, 1007, 1013 and 1001 struggle to get their coal train on the move as they climb away from the exchange sidings at Swan Lake AB, June 2001.
(John Chalcraft)

Former Northern Alberta RR, having been absorbed by Canadian National, is seen in June 1982 at Peace River AB, where a pair of SD40-2s headed by 5702, plus CN power, bring a train of tank cars round a sharp bend. (DC Collection)

CN C44-9W 2574 and SD75I 5717 enter the yards at Jasper AB with a westbound manifest freight train in May 2007. (Ian Francis)

Showing the results of mergers and locos of absorbed groups running far off their traditional beaten tracks, a CN eastbound container train enters Jasper AB behind SD70M-2 8856 and Illinois Central SD70 1018 in May 2010. (Ian Francis)

In the latest Rocky Mountaineer livery, GP40-2s 8011 and 8016 arrive at Jasper running late in June 2014. (Ian Francis)

With the snowcapped Rockies as a backdrop, train no 1, the westbound 'Canadian' heads south past Tete Jaune Cache BC in February 2005, behind a pair of VIA F40PH-2. (John Chalcraft)

Eight CN locos head a potash train over the North Thompson River in May 1986, at an undisclosed location in British Columbia. (DC Collection)

Train 104, a Vancouver to Montreal container train heads east past Hacienda Caballo BC behind CN SD751 5757, SD60F 5558 and SD40-2W 5322 in June 2001. The North Thompson River snakes through the valley. (John Chalcraft)

Approaching Kamloops from the north, CN SD70M-2s 8023 and 8017 with ex BCR SD40-2 750 pass Heffley Creek BC with a train of sulphur, August 2006.

CN C44-9W 2561 and SD60F 5516 head west with a container train at Tranquille BC in August 2006.

Loram rail grinding train RG 310 is stabled at Tranquille, ready for its next spell of work, probably during the night since it was seen stabled the following day at Wallachin.

What was a new class at the time, CN SD70M-2 8002 and ES44DC 2223 are eastbound at Tranquille with a twin stack container service.

CP CW44ACs 8755 and 9584 have a trainload of box cars in tow near Savona BC Seen heading west in August 2006.

The sun provides a slight glint on the following train near Savona. A local trip working with a variety of freight cars is hauled by CP SD40-2 5621, heading west.

At Wallachin BC, the CP line is on top of the escarpment, whilst the CN line follows the bank of the Thompson River. ON the CP line, CW44AC 9716 and SD90MAC 9154 speed past with an eastbound twin stack container train, banked in the rear by CW44AC 9784, well out of sight behind this lengthy consist, August 2006.

Dwarfed by the scenery, a CN container train creeps round the bends of the Thompson River at Wallachin, behind SD60F 5516 and C44-9W 2561.

An eastbound manifest freight trails round the bends, following CN SD40-2W 5246 and SD70M-2 8011. Wallachin, August 2006.

The Thompson River reflects the blue sky near Wallachin at the point where the CN line crosses the river in the background. A westbound twin stack container train is hauled by C44-9Ws 2585 and 2553.

Overlooking the road bridge giving access to Wallachin, the view includes CN SD75I 5723 hauling a lengthy eastbound manifest freight train. Careful observation of the top of the bridge girders below the taller tree show an osprey nest perched on the top. One would have thought a more comfortable location could have been found!

Approaching Ashcroft BC, the CN line hugs the river bank, where CN C44-9W 2534 and C40-8M 2408 work eastbound with a train of empty grain cars, August 2006.

On the other side of the river, CP CW44ACS 9817 and 9803 approach Ashcroft with a train of coal empties heading east. The bird by the pole didn't stop to have its portrait taken!

CP SD90MAC 9146 and CW44AC 9644 switch a trainload of cars carrying copper ore at Ashcroft.

South of Ashcroft BC, the CN and CP lines enter the Black Canyon with its spectacular scenery. The CP line on the east bank of the Thompson River hosts SD40-2s 5968 and 5733, and SD40-2Fs 9005 and 9023 on the approach to the town with an eastbound manifest freight train, June 2000. (John Chalcraft)

On the opposite bank, unidentified CN SD40-2 and C44-9W locos are leading an eastbound twin stack container train which snakes round the bends of the river.

With the CN line on the left, having crossed the river in the canyon, an empty CP coal train enters the tunnel with CW44AC 9756 bringing up the rear where the double track layout becomes single up to Ashcroft.

The CP and CN lines now parallel each other on the east bank of the Thompson River below Black Canyon, where a CN manifest freight heads east behind SD70M-2s 8023 and 8017 and ex BCR SD40-2 750, the same locos as were seen a few days earlier at Heffley Creek..

The CP single line having now cleared, a loaded potash train now exits the tunnel with ES44AC 8752 and CW44AC 8505 working steadily westwards.

Shortly afterwards, an eastbound container train comes to a halt behind CW44ACs 8547 and 9530, to await another westbound service.

How lucky can you get? Two for the price of one! With Hapag-Lloyd containers brightening the foreground, CN SD40-2 5382 and ES44DC 2226 work west with a container train, whilst alongside a CP coal train exits the tunnel behind CW44AC 9815. August 2006 in the Black Canyon BC.

From a high viewpoint looking down the valley from Black Canyon, the CP and CN tracks are seen, with a pair of CN C44-9Ws heading a never-ending twin stack container train heading east. In the distance is where the uni-directional arrangement of working starts, with trains heading east on one side of the river and vice versa, irrespective of which company's trains are operating.

A west bound CP container train behind CW44ACs 9552 and 9509 are seen alongside the Thompson River, a little way north of Spences Bridge BC in August 2006. This train is on the previously owned CP track.

Also on the CP track, CP CW44AC 8600 trails a loaded grain train.

On the other side of the river – the former CN line – a CP CW44AC works east with a train of empty grain cars, August 2006.

And if you are very lucky, you can get one photo with trains passing on the opposite sides of the river, as seen here at Spences Bridge BC in June 2000. Both trains are CP manifest freights, that closest behind SD90MACs 9150 and 9103, the other behind SD40-2F 9013 and SD40-2 5990. (John Chalcraft)

At Thompson BC in June 2000, on the former CN tracks, an eastbound CP manifest freight is hauled by CW44ACs 8526 and 9572. (John Chalcraft)

On the other bank at Thompson, a CN container train heads west towards its destination at Vancouver behind C44-9Ws 2610 and 2632 in August 2006. The difficulty in constructing the line within the confines left available for the Canadian National are apparent.

The same train is seen slightly further on at Pitquah BC, passing a manifest freight held in the siding. Looking at the side of the cutting, it is no wonder that avalanche shelters have been constructed in various places along this line.

In the days before uni-directional working commenced, CN SD50F stands at Boston Bar BC with a long train of empty grain cars before leaving as seen in the next two photos, August 1999.

Now heading east on its own CN tracks from Boston Bar, the train curves round the embankment on the east side, while lack of space requires the other track to be built on a viaduct.

At Cisco BC, the Canadian Pacific line crosses from one side of the Fraser River to the other, having been built first, and so able to choose the best route. Consequently, the Canadian National had to make do with second best. The CN train is seen on the bridge moving to the opposite side of the river, going over the top of the CP bridge, the girders of which can be seen in the bottom left.

Coming to a halt at North Bend (on the opposite bank to Boston Bar BC), CP CW44ACs 9538 and 9522 are at the head of yet another train with coal for export at Roberts Bank, August 1999.

An eastbound container train passes track workers at Spuzzum BC behind CP CW33ACs 9666 and 9675.

Following the gorge of the Fraser River, the same train is seen broadside on at Hell's Gate, clinging to the cliff face. Both locos carry the recently introduced beaver symbol.

Having chased the train, it is seen in a final shot approaching the bridge at Cisco. All three shots taken in August 1999.

At the end of the uni-directional arrangements, CN C44-9W 2591 and C40-8M 2423 head west to their final destination with yet one more coal train. The train is seen at Chilliwack BC in August 2006.

Entering the intermodal yard at Pitt Meadows BC, on the outskirts of the Vancouver metropolitan area, CP SD90MACs 9131 and 9137 are heading a mixed train of containers and auto racks, April 2001.

The Esquimalt and Nanaimo RR (subsequently owned by Rail America and Southern Railway of British Columbia) operated freight services on Vancouver Island until March 2011, but these locomotives had already been transferred to the mainland and operated by CP. Acting as yard switchers at the Pitt Meadow facility, GP38s 3005 and 3004 show off their unique colour scheme in August 1999.

With the lead locomotive carrying United Way emblems, CP SD90MAC 9159, CEFX SD90MAC 134, SD90MAC 9302 and SD40-2 5966 struggle to get going with an empty grain train, heading east at Pitt Meadows after leaving Coquitlam yards in April 2001.

A limited passenger service operates between Vancouver and Mission BC, operated by West Coast Express. In August 1999, F59PHI 905, with its train of five double deck coaches exits the bridge over the Pitt River on its way to Mission.

The major CP loco shed at Coquitlam outside Vancouver, is host to locomotives and other residents, which will no doubt keep the cleaners at the facility busy! In two different liveries, CW44ACs 8532 and 9577 take a rest before their next spell of duties, August 1999.

CP GP9 1582 switches the western end of Coquitlam yards with an interesting mix of cars in September 1991.

CP GP35s 5024 and 5013 plus three others leave Coquitlam and head downtown in a cloud of exhaust smoke with a manifest freight in September 1991.

CP GP9 8217, GP30 5000 and GP35 5027 switch tank cars at Port Moody BC in September 1991.

CP SD40-1s 5414 and 5403 enter the terminal area at Vancouver BC with a container train, passing stabled West Coast Express trains, no doubt waiting for the evening rush hour services, August 1999.

Posed by the market at New Westminster BC, on the left CP GP38AC 3001 and on the right Southern Railway of British Columbia SD38AC 381 and SD38-2 382, September 1991.

CN SD40-2Ws 5321, 5338 and 5287 plus GP9 7209 work a transfer freight to BC Rail in North Vancouver. New Westminster in September 1999.

Also at New Westminster, CN SD40-2W 5291, SD40 5152 plus two others approach with another transfer freight from BC Rail, passing GP9 7222 which is parked with a short local freight.

Vancouver passenger terminal in September 1999, where the eastbound 'Canadian' is formed in two sections. On the left, the main section, train No 2, is headed by VIA F40PH-2s 6401 and 6412, while on the right the second portion is headed by 6448 plus one other. Since it was well before time for the trains to depart and passengers were not due to board, I had to use persuasive powers to gain access to take this photo!

The Skytrain system serves various areas of Vancouver, much of it above ground level. Train no. 090 is seen at New Westminster station in September 1999.

Perfectly positioned in the middle of the bridge over the Fraser River, a Skytrain makes its way to downtown Vancouver. The next bridge carries a road, and that most distant is the CN rail bridge over the river.

CN GP9 7243 plus slug are stabled in North Vancouver with a train of tank cars, April 2001.

CN GP9rm 7205 with slug 214 switch a variety of freight cars in North Vancouver in August 1999.

A rare Alco S6 switcher no. 81, owned by Neptune Bulk Terminal is stabled with Helm SW1500 1512 and an NPT slug in North Vancouver, August 1999.

In the same area, Vancouver Wharves SW1500 821 goes about its switching duties.

Glinting in the morning sun, BC Rail RS18 627 and slug 5403 are switching their North Vancouver yard, September 1991.

BC Rail operated tourist trains to Squamish hauled by ex Canadian Pacific 'Royal Hudson' 2860. The 4-6-4 is seen in steam at North Vancouver in September 1991.

BC Rail CRS20 CAT 601 stands in the loco shed yard in North Vancouver, specially painted in Pacific Starlight livery for tourist train purposes. When I commented on the number of lights on the front end, I was told 'Remember you are in Canada – half of them are English and half French!'

One for the modellers – a rear view of the loco.

BC Rail Budd RDC3 no. 11, used on services to Lillooet BC, stands in the shed yard at North Vancouver, April 2001.

One of BC Rail's newest acquisitions, C44-9WL 4651 is clean, but not very colourful. It is seen at North Vancouver with other locos in the normal three-colour livery in April 2001.

Another BC Rail tourist train was the 'Whistler Northwind', which had a train set specially painted to suit. It is stabled in North Vancouver, headed by B39-8 1700 in April 2001.

A train of sulphur empties enters the yards at North Vancouver behind BC Rail C40-8Ms 4603 and 4620 plus SD40-2 754, April 2001.

Carrying Americana Film inscriptions, BC Rail M420W 647 approaches Squamish BC with a filming special in August 1999.

The clouds hang over the hills at Squamish, where a BC Rail manifest freight train is about to leave for the north behind C40-8M 4623, SD40-2 746 and C44-9WL 9643 in August 1999.

A northbound train of wood products is seen near Whistler BC behind three BC Rail C40-8Ms in November 2002. (DC Collection)

A pair of BC Rail C40-8Ms snake a manifest freight through the spectacular countryside near Lillooet BC in July 1991. (DC Collection)

Also near Lillooet, the train of containers is dwarfed as it heads south behind two more BC Rail C40-8Ms. (DC Collection)

Coal operations in the Tumbler Ridge area of BC ceased in 2011, but in September 1986 trains were worked by electric locomotives. Class GF6C 6002 and 6001 are seen at a coal loading point at Quintette. (DC Collection)

VIA operated Vancouver Island services from Victoria to Courtenay until 2011 when the trains were suspended. In June 2008, a pair of Budd RDCs, led by no. 6133 pass over the lifting bridge outside Victoria station with the 0800 service. (Ian Francis).

The Duluth, Winnipeg and Pacific is a wholly owned CN subsidiary. One of their SD40 locos 5903 leads Grand Trunk and CN locos hauling a manifest freight at London ON in September 1997. (DC Collection)

CN SD40-2W 5313 and EMD GP40-2 run light engines under Tifft Street Bridge south of Buffalo NY in June 1994.

CN SD40s 5019 and 5219 head towards Chicago passing through Eola Yards IL with a manifest freight train in May 1993.

Exercising its trackage rights at Rochelle IL, a westbound manifest freight on the BNSF main line from Chicago to the Twin Cities and North West, crosses the UP main line from Chicago to the west in May 1997. The motive power is CN SD75I 5714, GP40-2L 9440 and SD40 5041.

CN GP40 6417, LMS C40-8W 736 and NREX SD40 869 add to the variety at La Grange IL where they head south with a manifest freight in May 1997. The lead loco carries the North America map colour scheme, and was originally a Detroit, Toledo and Ironton RR engine, subsequently taken over by Grand Trunk Western and then in turn by Canadian National.

Trundling along below the bluffs at St Paul MN, CN SD40-2 52xx (the cab side was too dirty to get the full number), EML SD40-2 6403 and CN SD40 5027 work south with a manifest freight in May 1997. The St Paul high rise buildings dominate the skyline, and the Minnesota state capitol building is seen on the right, May 1997.

CN SD40 5041 and Helm (ex Detroit Edison) 5004 work northwards with a manifest freight past the yards south of St Paul.

CN SD70I 5621 and SD75I 5626 speed past some grain silos at Leeds IL, on the BNSF main line from Chicago to Galesburg, in April 1999 with a northbound manifest freight train.

Wisconsin Central was acquired by CN in 2001, including its operations elsewhere in the world. In their distinctive colour scheme SD40-2 6002 and SD45 7520 stand in the yards at Fond Du Lac, WI in April 1999. The lead loco was originally owned by Algoma Central RR which ran north from Sault Ste. Marie into Ontario, which was taken over by WC in 1995.

A Wisconsin Central loco has escaped its normal territory. SD45 6517, leading BN SD40 6526, seen heading north with a coal train at Madisonville KY in May 1993.

Wisconsin Central acquired the UK freight and mail operations after British Rail had been privatised and established the new company as English, Welsh & Scottish Railways (EWS). They quickly introduced the EMD London ON built JT42CWR class 66, two of which are seen at Cholsey, Berks, in September 2004, where 66144 heads north with a Southampton to Ditton container service, overtaking 66033 with a Marchwood to Didcot train.

The class 92s were built for traffic working through the Channel Tunnel, although in the event, very little materialised, and the locos worked in other areas of electrified track. In July 2007, 92031 'The Institute of Logistics and Transport' hauled a Wembley to Trafford Park intermodal past South Kenton.

In 2009, EWS was taken over by DB Schenker of Germany. Seen in their colours, but named in commemoration of the Canadian CEO of EWS Keith Heller, 67018 was also emblazoned with a maple leaf, and is seen departing Banbury in February 2014, with a train from Birmingham Moor Street to London Marylebone.

A pair of Grand Trunk locos, GP40-2 6417 and SD40-2 5936 run light engines through Highlands IL, in the western suburbs of Chicago, no doubt on their way to the yards at Eola to pick up a train, May 1997.

The Illinois Central had sold and then taken back the line from Chicago to Dubuque IA, being operated by Chicago Central & Pacific in the interim. At Seward IL, an IC manifest freight works west behind GP38-2 9604, GP38 2006, still in CCP colours, and IC GP3802 9627, May 1997.

Fulton KY is a hub on the Illinois Central, where GT GP38-2 5846 and IC GP38-2 9624, both now part of CN, back down onto a northbound freight train in April 1999.

The Illinois Central RR was acquired by CN, with interchange of locomotives starting from 1999. Still operating in its old guise, IC SD70s 1002 and 1018 approach Fulton KY with a New Orleans to Chicago manifest freight in April 1999.

Sitting peacefully on shed at East Binghamton NY in June 1994, CP SD40 5406 heads Helm (ex GTI) GP40-2 502, GATX SD40-2 7362, GATX (ex UP) SD40-2 2008 and CP SD40-2 5647.

CP took over the Delaware & Hudson RR in 1991, but still in the original owner's colours in June 1994 was GP38-2 7307 seen switching a Southern box car at Binghamton NY.

In the mid-1990s, CP set up a subsidiary group for accounting purposes identified as the St Lawrence and Hudson – it ceased in 2001 reverting to conventional CP. Seen freshly painted with its StL & H logos, SD40-2 5651 and CP SD40 5500 pass La Grange IL with a northbound manifest freight.

CP – with the full CP Rail system caption – MP15AC 1404 switches the yard at St Paul MN in May 1997.

One for the modellers, to show what the top of an EMD switcher looks like.

Seen across containers on a BNSF twin stack service at Tifft Street, Buffalo NY, SOO line SD60s 6012 and 6025 head north with a TOFC intermodal train stretching into the distance, working on the NS owned, ex Nickel Plate tracks, June 1994.

The bearded conductor of SOO line GP38-2 4403 glares at me as the train, a southbound TOFC intermodal passes La Grange IL in May 1997, adding to the variety at this busy location.

Getting further away from home territory, SOO SD40-2 772, Helm GP40-2 4000 and CP SD40-2 5955 are stabled on the CSX loco shed at Hamlet NC in the company of CSX GP38-2 2666 in October 1997. The local enthusiasts were quite taken aback by the appearance of these engines, which were required for a special working, which can be seen in the companion volume *Rails Across North America*.

Getting about as far south in the USA as can be for a SOO line locomotive, SD60 6053 keeps company with SP SD45 8674 on shed at Victoria TX in November 1995. Another view for modellers to show details of the rear end of this class.